Tell Me

TELL ME

❧

POEMS BY
KIM ADDONIZIO

BOA Editions, Ltd. ❧ Rochester, NY ❧ 2000

LC #: 00-131756

ISBN: 1-880238-91-8 paper

01 02 03   7 6 5 4

Publications by BOA Editions, Ltd.—
a not-for-profit corporation under section 501 (c) (3)
of the United States Internal Revenue Code—
are made possible with the assistance of grants from
the Literature Program of the New York State Council on the Arts,
the Literature Program of the National Endowment for the Arts,
the Sonia Raiziss Giop Charitable Foundation,
the Eric Mathieu King Fund of The Academy of American Poets,
The Halcyon Hill Foundation, Starbucks Foundation, as well as from
the Mary S. Mulligan Charitable Trust, the County of Monroe, NY,
and the Estate of E.M.K.

*   *   *

See page 96 for special individual acknowledgments.

Cover Design: Lisa Mauro/Mauro Design
Typesetting: Richard Foerster
Manufacturing: McNaughton & Gunn, Lithographers
BOA Logo: Mirko

BOA Editions, Ltd.
Steven Huff, Publisher
Richard Garth, Chair, Board of Directors
A. Poulin, Jr., President & Founder (1976–1996)
260 East Avenue
Rochester, NY 14604
www.boaeditions.org

for Dorianne

Let us sing together: know? We know nothing.
....
The light illuminates nothing, and the wise man teaches nothing.
What does human language say? What does the water in the rock say?

—Antonio Machado, *Proverbios y cantares*,
translated by Robert Bly

Contents

4. Good Girl

1.

The Singing

THE NUMBERS

How many nights have I lain here like this, feverish with plans,
with fears, with the last sentence someone spoke, still trying to
    finish
a conversation already over? How many nights were wasted
in not sleeping, how many in sleep—I don't know
how many hungers there are, how much radiance or salt, how
    many times
the world breaks apart, disintegrates to nothing and starts up
    again
in the course of an ordinary hour. I don't know how God can bear
seeing everything at once: the falling bodies, the monuments and
    burnings,
the lovers pacing the floors of how many locked hearts. I want to
    close
my eyes and find a quiet field in fog, a few sheep moving toward a
    fence.
I want to count them, I want them to end. I don't want to wonder
how many people are sitting in restaurants about to close down,
which of them will wander the sidewalks all night
while the pies revolve in the refrigerated dark. How many days
are left of my life, how much does it matter if I manage to say
one true thing about it—how often have I tried, how often
failed and fallen into depression? The field is wet, each grassblade
gleaming with its own particularity, even here, so that I can't help
asking again, the white sky filling with footprints, bricks,
with mutterings over rosaries, with hands that pass over flames
before covering the eyes. I'm tired, I want to rest now.
I want to kiss the body of my lover, the one mouth, the simple
    name
without a shadow. Let me go. How many prayers
are there tonight, how many of us must stay awake and listen?

THE SINGING

There's a bird crying outside, or maybe calling, anyway it goes on
    and on
without stopping, so I begin to think it's *my* bird, my insistent
I, I, I that today is so trapped by some nameless but still relentless
    longing
that I can't get any further than this, one note clicking
    metronomically
in the afternoon silence, measuring out some possible melody
I can't begin to learn. I could say it's the bird of my loneliness
asking, as usual, for love, for more anyway than I have; I could as
    easily call it
grief, ambition, knot of self that won't untangle, fear of my own
    heart. All
I can do is listen to the way it keeps on, as if it's enough just to
    launch a voice
against stillness, even a voice that says so little, that no one is
    likely to answer
with anything but sorrow, and their own confusion. *I, I, I,* isn't it
    the sweetest
sound, the beautiful, arrogant ego refusing to disappear? I don't
    know
what I want, only that I'm desperate for it, that I can't stop asking.
    That when
the bird finally quiets I need to say it doesn't, that all afternoon
I hear it, and into the evening; that even now, in the darkness, it
    goes on.

GLASS

In every bar there's someone sitting alone and absolutely absorbed
by whatever he's seeing in the glass in front of him,
a glass that looks ordinary, with something clear or dark
inside it, something partially drunk but never completely gone.
Everything's there: all the plans that came to nothing,
the stupid love affairs, and the terrifying ones, the ones where
    actual happiness
opened like a hole beneath his feet and he fell in, then lay helpless
while the dirt rained down a little at a time to bury him.
And his friends are there, cracking open six-packs, raising the
    bottles,
the click of their meeting like the sound of a pool cue
nicking a ball, the wrong ball, that now edges, black and shining,
toward the waiting pocket. But it stops short, and at the bar the
    lone drinker
signals for another. Now the relatives are floating up
with their failures, with cancer, with plateloads of guilt
and a little laughter, too, and even beauty—some afternoon from
    childhood,
a lake, a ball game, a book of stories, a few flurries of snow
that thicken and gradually cover the earth until the whole
world's gone white and quiet, until there's hardly a world
at all, no traffic, no money or butchery or sex,
just a blessed peace that seems final but isn't. And finally
the glass that contains and spills this stuff continually
while the drinker hunches before it, while the bartender gathers
up empties, gives back the drinker's own face. Who knows what it
    looks like;
who cares whether or not it was young once, or ever lovely,
who gives a shit about some drunk rising to stagger toward
the bathroom, some man or woman or even lost
angel who recklessly threw it all over—heaven, the ether,
the celestial works—and said, *Fuck it, I want to be human?*
Who believes in angels, anyway? Who has time for anything
but their own pleasures and sorrows, for the few good people

they've managed to gather around them against the uncertainty,
against afternoons of sitting alone in some bar
with a name like the Embers or the Ninth Inning or the Wishing
    Well?
Forget that loser. Just tell me who's buying, who's paying;
Christ but I'm thirsty, and I want to tell you something,
come close I want to whisper it, to pour
the words burning into you, the same words for each one of you,
listen, it's simple, I'm saying it now, while I'm still sober,
while I'm not about to weep bitterly into my own glass,
while you're still here—don't go yet, stay, stay,
give me your shoulder to lean against, steady me, don't let me
    drop,
I'm so in love with you I can't stand up.

QUANTUM

You know how hard it is sometimes just to walk on the streets
    downtown, how everything enters you
the way the scientists describe it—photons streaming through
    bodies, caroming off the air, the impenetrable brick
of buildings an illusion—sometimes you can feel how porous you
    are, how permeable, and the man lurching in circles
on the sidewalk, cutting the space around him with a tin can and
    saying *Uhh! Uhhhh! Uhh!* over and over
is part of it, and the one in gold chains leaning against the glass of
    the luggage store is, and the one who steps toward you
from his doorway, meaning to ask something apparently simple,
    like *What's the time*, something you know
you can no longer answer; he's part of it, the body of the world
    which is also yours and which keeps insisting
you recognize it. And the trouble is, you do, but it's happening
    here, among the crowds and exhaust smells,
and you taste every greasy scrap of paper, the globbed spit you
    step over, your tongue is as thick with dirt
as though you've fallen on your hands and knees to lick the oil-
    scummed street, as sour as if you've been drinking
the piss of those men passing their bottle in the little park with its
    cement benches and broken fountain. And it's no better
when you descend the steps to the Metro and some girl's wailing
    off-key about her heart—your heart—
over the awful buzzing of the strings, and you hurry through the
    turnstile, fumbling out the money that's passed
from how many hands into yours, getting rid of all your change
    except one quarter you're sure she sees
lying blind in your pocket as you get into a car and the doors seal
    themselves behind you. But still it isn't over.
Because later, when you're home, looking out your window at the
    ocean, at the calm of the horizon line,
and the apple in your hand glows in that golden light that happens
    in the afternoon, suffusing you with something
you're sure is close to peace, you think of the boy bagging

groceries at Safeway, of how his face was flattened
in a way that was familiar—bootheel of a botched chromosome—
    and you remember his canceled blue eyes,
and his hands, flaking, rash-reddened, that lifted each thing and
    caressed it before placing it carefully
in your sack, and the monotonous song he muttered, *paper or*
    plastic, paper or plastic, his mouth slack,
a teardrop of drool at the corner; and you know he's a part of it
    too, raising the fruit to your lips you look out
at the immense and meaningless blue and know you're inside it,
    you realize you're eating him now.

THEODICY

Suppose we could see evil with such clarity we wouldn't hesitate
to stamp it out like stray sparks from a fire. Look at those boys
shooting baskets in the park, jostling each other to hook the ball
through the iron circle at the end of the asphalt—what if you knew

a secret about one of them? Shirtless, he stands vibrating
at the edge of an imaginary line, the orange globe trembling
at the tips of his fingers, sweat drawing the light into his skin—
what if he'd done something unspeakable, something I can't

talk about but know you can imagine, to the one
you love most in this world? Your child, maybe,
or the person whose body you know so well you can see it
simply by closing your eyes— What if he'd broken that body;

do you think if I handed you a gun you would walk up
to that shining boy and use it? You might think first
that maybe he couldn't help himself, maybe he was trying
as he stood there concentrating on his shot to stop the noise

of some relentless machine grinding away in his brain,
the same one you hear in yours sometimes, bearing down until
you can't tell what's true anymore, or good. Suppose God
began to have that trouble. Suppose the first man

turned out cruel and stupid, a cartoon creature
that farted and giggled continuously; suppose the woman ripped
saplings from the earth all day and refused to speak
or be grateful for anything. What if they decided to torment

the smaller, weaker beasts, and just as God was about
to strike them dead and start over they turned toward each other
and discovered fucking, and the serpent whispered *Look at them*
and God's head filled with music while the wild sparks leaped

from their bodies, bright as the new stars in the heavens.

TARGET

It feels so good to shoot a gun,
to stand with your legs apart
holding a nine millimeter in both hands
aiming at something that can't run.
Over and over I rip holes

in the paper target clamped to its hanger,
target I move closer with the flick of a switch
or so far away its center looks
like a small black planet in its white square
of space. It feels good to nestle a clip

of bullets against the heel of your hand,
to ratchet one into the chamber
and cock the hammer back and fire, the recoil
surging along your arms as the muzzle kicks up, as you keep
control. It's so good you no longer wonder

why some boys lift them from bottom drawers and boxes
at the backs of closets, and drive fast into lives
they won't finish, lean from their car windows and
let go a few rounds into whatever's out there.
You can hear what comes back as they speed away:

burst glass, or the high ring of struck steel,
or maybe moans. Now you want
to take the thing and hurl it into
the ocean, to wait until it drops down
through the dark and cold and lodges so deep

nothing could retrieve it. But you know it would
float back and wash up like a bottle
carrying a message from a dead man.
You stand there firing until the gun feels
light again, and innocent. And then you reload.

SALMON

In this shallow creek
they flop and writhe forward as the dead
float back toward them. Oh, I know

what I should say: fierce burning in the body
as her eggs burst free, milky cloud
of sperm as he quickens them. I should stand

on the bridge with my camera,
frame the white froth of rapids where one
arcs up for an instant in its final grace.

But I have to go down among
the rocks the glacier left
and squat at the edge of the water

where a stinking pile of them lies,
where one crow balances and sinks
its beak into a gelid eye.

I have to study the small holes
gouged into their skin, their useless gills,
their gowns of black flies. I can't

make them sing. I want to,
but all they do is open
their mouths a little wider

so the water pours in
until I feel like I'm drowning.
On the bridge the tour bus waits

and someone waves, and calls down
It's time, and the current keeps lifting
dirt from the bottom to cover the eggs.

A CHILDHOOD

Our drinks came with paper umbrellas.
My mother put on tennis whites.
My father went to the bar
the way he always did.

My mother put on tennis whites.
My brother threw me against a wall
the way he always did.
I believed in my guardian angel.

My brother threw my mother against a wall.
I walked in my sleep.
I believed in my guardian angel.
I woke up far from the house.

I walked in my sleep.
My mother read fairy tales and sang to me.
I woke up far from the house.
My mother was old, my father dead.

My mother read fairy tales and sang to me.
My father and brother crashed through the door.
My mother was old, my father dead
along with my guardian angel.

My father and brother crashed through the door.
I went to the bar
along with my guardian angel
and our drinks came with paper umbrellas.

☙

THE MOMENT

The way my mother bent to her car door, fumbling the keys,
    taking forever it seemed
to find the right one, line it up with the lock and feebly push it in
    and turn,
the way she opened the door so slowly, bending a bit more, easing
    herself finally into the leather seat— She'd hurt her ribs, she
    explained, but it wasn't injury
that I saw, not the temporary setback that's followed by healing,
    the body's tenacious renewal;
I saw for the first time old age, decline, the inevitable easing
    toward death. Once in the car, though,
settled behind the wheel, backing out and heading for the steady
    traffic on the highway,
she was herself again, my mother as I'd always known her: getting
    older, to be sure,
in her seventies now, but still vital, still the athlete she'd been all
    her life; jogging, golf,
tennis especially—the sport she'd excelled at, racking up
    championships—they were as natural
to her as breath. All my life she'd been the definition of grace, of a
    serenely unshakable confidence
in the body; impossible ever to imagine her helpless, frail, confined
    to walker or wheelchair.
She was humming now as she drove, that momentary fumbling
    erased, no trace of it.
No acknowledgment of pain, of the ache she must still be feeling
    in her side. My mother
refused all that, she would go on refusing it. She peered ahead at
    the busy road, the past all but forgotten—
somewhere behind us griefs, losses, terrible knowledge, but ahead
    of us a day we'd spend together,
we were going there now, while there was still time, none of it was
    going to be wasted.

❧

GARBAGE

Don't think about where it goes
after you tie it up in its white bag and squash it down
into the can dragged out to the curb. Don't think
of the stink of the truck backing up, or the men in their filthy
    gloves
hanging off the sides, cursing in the near-dark of a new day
in which, somewhere, someone is about to be thrown into a cell
the way garbage is thrown into a deep pit for burning,
the way bodies are thrown in to be shoveled over.
Don't think about the dump, the scavenging rats,
the reeking piles they tunnel through—the flattened shoes,
the dolls with their eyes torn out, the pennies, the lost
wedding ring, whatever's found its way there and won't return
except as a stain, a bad smell on the air, a poison
seeding the clouds until it rains back down. But today
the weather's lovely; look at the sky, its purity,
its nullity, only gulls crossing it on their way
to the beaches. Don't let the gulls remind you
of how they dive beak-first into fish, of fish floating up with the
    sewage.
Especially don't think of dead things, or of vultures, how they wait
    so patiently
while something is bleeding into the dirt, and then jostle each
    other
as they hunch black-frocked around it, feeding the way everyone
    feeds;
oh, don't think now of all the food you've wasted,
scraped off plates or gone bad on the shelf, in the fridge,
you couldn't help it, you meant to save everyone, the children
    especially,
but it keeps filling up the house: the thick black print of
    newspapers,
the petitions for money with lists of their names, their actual faces,
they're still alive, they're out there with the guards
and the soldiers and the flies, so don't think of how clean

your house is, don't think for a minute you've gotten it all,
look at your hands, they're covered with it, you can try
to wash them or else plunge them in; even one finger, take it and
     scrape
up a little of the sludge and the muck and the stench
of the human, feel how the barest hope clings there.

THINGS THAT DON'T HAPPEN

Is there a place they go—the gold stalks, the umbels, the new
   shoots,
when the seeds rot in the fields or are eaten by birds? Is there a city
   someone meant to build
where your car is humming steadily through the streets, while here
   the ignition
turns over with a dull sound announcing silence, and you trudge
   back to the house,
the appointment canceled, erased from the date book, and a
   different day starts, the way
it starts for someone in a farmhouse kitchen, with a mother who's
   suddenly
a widow, an uncle who says *Don't let any niggers touch him* so
   that for a moment
the black coroner lays out the body, and gently closes the eyes
while the wife slips on her old nightgown and the son whispers on
   the phone
to his lover, and the monsignor prepares his eulogy—
this is a eulogy for the things that don't happen, for the stillborn,
the unstamped passport, the ring given back or pawned, or simply
   tossed
into a drawer with the final papers, the ones that say you failed
as everything fails, while each day the tiny accumulations, the
   insignificant actions,
destroy those shimmerings in the air, those sparks thrown off, the
   fire of the actual
consuming everything. The ice settles in the empty glass beside my
   bed, a sudden,
startling *click*, a latch, an opening or closing, I can't tell which; I
   could get up, pour
another shot, stop trying to explain how it obsesses me, each day
the *not* of what is: this lover's mouth and not the last one's, this
   dream
that isn't premonition and vanishes on waking, incoherency
   refusing

to coalesce, the words stoppered in a bottle that floats to the
    horizon's edge
and goes down, flaring for an instant. And each day the terror,
    your house
with its blood-smirched doorpost, the angel passing over but
    stopping somewhere else:
brains sprayed on a brick wall or leaking into the dirt, bodies in
    the river carried down
with the current, river where one fish feels a hook tearing through
    its gills and rises
frantically into the air. But why should we be sad; shouldn't we be
    breaking out
the champagne, thinking of the would-be suicide sweating in a
    room, the pistol
with its rusted firing pin flung onto the bed, all the black shoes
    safe in the back
of the closet; and of the boy in Birkenau, his death that doesn't
    happen
so that two generations later, in Brooklyn, a girl can kneel down
to place a small stone on his stone, and stand to brush the dirt off
    her knees?
Isn't the loss held in abeyance each day, the benign tumor, the
    wreckage
at the intersection where you might have been standing, except
    that you caught the streetcar;
but really there is no streetcar, none of this is happening—it's
    trying to but I can't help
realizing how hopeless it is: as fast as I have you step up, pay the
    fare,
struggle into a seat with your packages, I've kept you from a
    thousand better things.
I should let you lie in bed late at night, awake but not alone; I
    should nestle you
against the one true lover you haven't let yourself long for in years
but who is finally here, who's not ever leaving. I should seal you
    up
with the breast, the kiss. Nightingale, nipple, tongue dipping into
    the real,

the taste of it, the singing, the virtual lark, the light beginning but
  not yet
day, not clothes yet, not shame or betrayal, just the lovers too
  unironic to survive
anywhere but here. So this is the end, because I want to keep my
  stupid faith
in romance, in the idea of love, and if you would just let it go on
  forever this way
you wouldn't have to go out into the nothing where something is
  waiting
especially for you, though what it is I can't tell you, only that it
  begins
as soon as you stop listening, and turn away, only that it happens
  now.

HA

A man walks into a bar. You think that's some kind of joke?
Actually he runs in, to get out of the freezing weather.
Who cares? you say. Nobody you know.
You've got your own troubles, could use a drink yourself.
You get your coat, a long scarf. You trudge
to the corner over the scraped sidewalk, slip and fall down
on the ice. Actually a banana peel, but who's looking?
Only a priest, a rabbi, and a lawyer you vaguely recognize—
didn't she help with the divorce? Never mind, the marriage
is over, good riddance. You're thinking now
you'd better have a double. You get up, holding your hip,
and limp toward the neon martini glass.
Anyway a man goes into a bar, just like you do.
He's tired of life, tired of being alone. No one
takes him seriously; at work he's the butt of jokes,
the foreman calls him *Moron* all day long. It's true
he's not too bright. He wants to kill himself,
but doesn't know how to. He orders drink after drink,
cursing the angel who passed out brains.
You take the stool next to him. In half an hour
you're pals—two losers getting shitfaced.
You start to tell each other riddles. What's big and red
and eats rocks; what do you get when you cross a penis
with a potato? Why is there something rather than nothing?
If God is good, how is it that the weed of evil
takes root everywhere, and what is there to keep us
from murdering each other in despair? Why is pleasure always
a prelude to pain? The bartender takes your glasses, tells you
it's time to get out. You stumble through the door,
and there you are in the cold and the wind and a little snow
that's started to fall. Two losers stand on a corner.
One turns to the other and says, Why did our love end?
The other can't answer. Why do they torment me? he says.
The snowstorm begins in earnest but still they stand there,
determined to stay put until they finally get it.

NIGHT OF THE LIVING, NIGHT OF THE DEAD

When the dead rise in movies they're hideous
and slow. They stagger uphill toward the farmhouse
like drunks headed home from the bar.
Maybe they only want to lie down inside
while some room spins around them, maybe that's why
they bang on the windows while the living
hammer up boards and count out shotgun shells.
The living have plans: to get to the pickup parked
in the yard, to drive like hell to the next town.
The dead with their leaky brains,
their dangling limbs and ruptured hearts,
are sick of all that. They'd rather stumble
blind through the field until they collide
with a tree, or fall through a doorway
like they're the door itself, sprung from its hinges
and slammed flat on the linoleum. That's the life
for a dead person: *wham, wham, wham*
until you forget your name, your own stinking
face, the reason you jolted awake
in the first place. Why are you here,
whatever were you hoping as you lay
in your casket like a dumb clarinet?
You know better now. The sound track's depressing
and the living hate your guts. Come closer
and they'll show you how much. *Wham, wham, wham,*
you're killed again. Thank God this time
they're burning your body, thank God
it can't drag you around anymore
except in nightmares, late-night reruns
where you lift up the lid, and crawl out
once more, and start up the hill toward the house.

SIAMESE

They were teenaged girls, joined, it appeared, just above the right eyebrow of each, so that they faced opposite directions. The one facing forward carried her smaller sister, or else wheeled her on a kind of cart. Let's call them Sarah and Tarah; I've forgotten their names, and the name of the TV show that brought them into the hotel room where my best friend and I were watching. This was years ago, in high school, before either of us got married and divorced, before she found the tumor that turned out to be malignant, inoperable. Sarah's dream was to be a country singer. Maybe that was the kind of show it was, fulfilling people's fantasies, or maybe these two were famous for living so long past the point such twins usually do. Everything was arranged for Sarah: recording studio, session men, everyone in headphones, smiling, her sister on camera saying bashfully, "Don't look at me, it's *her* big night." Then the awful, heartfelt singing, followed by a promise from our host that next we'd follow Sarah and Tarah out for a night on the town. My friend and I exchanged a look. We jumped up and put our heads together, and lurched around the room—into the TV, the coffee table, between the matching beds, through the sliding glass door to the balcony. Do I need to tell you how hysterical we were? From the street, looking up, you might have thought we were the real thing.

VIRGIN SPRING

It's a terrible scene, the two men talking to the girl who foolishly
    lets them lead her away
from the road she's taking to church, the men raping and killing
    her, the young boy with them
watching, then left for a while with her body. But the film's next
    scene is more terrible
in some ways, the men and boy arriving at the house where the
    girl's parents live, but not
knowing, and the parents not knowing, either, offering a meal, all
    of them sitting together, breaking
bread at a long table— Is that the most awful, or is it when one
    man tries to sell the mother
her murdered daughter's clothes?— and she takes them, pretending
    to consider. Though how
could she pretend at that moment, how control herself? Yet she
    does; she goes outside,
locking them in the barn, and runs to her husband, to whom the
    task of killing them falls.
So it goes on—rape, betrayal, murder, not even the boy is spared.
    And what about the father,
swearing to build a church on the spot his daughter was killed,
    and the miracle of the water
gushing forth from the ground when they lift her body—Is that
    enough, is there some sort
of balance now, good following evil, revenge annulled, the family
    cleansed? What about
the other, dark-haired sister, the pregnant one, who had been a few
    yards behind on the road
to church that morning, who had followed the men and watched
    from a safe distance
while they erased the girl, her prettiness, her spoiled ways, her
    stupid innocence—

I don't know what to make of the sister. She's the one who knows
     the world is brutal
and goes on, scattering seed for the hogs, the one who says
     nothing, the one who survives.

THERAPY

My brother's in the house. I close my door.
He's in the kitchen. Bottles, knives. He breaks the lock,
drags me by one arm across the floor.
A small bird thrums its wings inside the clock;
now it's coming out, it's keeping track
of each indignity: that helpless day,
my father's drinking—Christ, the whole sick
drama of my childhood's on display
like a document in a museum. And you
sit listening, and nodding, like those toys
I've seen, their heads on springs. It's too
ridiculous, this ordering the noise
the past makes into music. What's it for?
Time's up. You're in the house. I'm through the door.

NEW YEAR'S DAY

The rain this morning falls
on the last of the snow

and will wash it away. I can smell
the grass again, and the torn leaves

being eased down into the mud.
The few loves I've been allowed

to keep are still sleeping
on the West Coast. Here in Virginia

I walk across the fields with only
a few young cows for company.

Big-boned and shy,
they are like girls I remember

from junior high, who never
spoke, who kept their heads

lowered and their arms crossed against
their new breasts. Those girls

are nearly forty now. Like me,
they must sometimes stand

at a window late at night, looking out
on a silent backyard, at one

rusting lawn chair and the sheer walls
of other people's houses.

They must lie down some afternoons
and cry hard for whoever used

to make them happiest,
and wonder how their lives

have carried them
this far without ever once

explaining anything. I don't know
why I'm walking out here

with my coat darkening
and my boots sinking in, coming up

with a mild sucking sound
I like to hear. I don't care

where those girls are now.
Whatever they've made of it

they can have. Today I want
to resolve nothing.

I only want to walk
a little longer in the cold

blessing of the rain,
and lift my face to it.

GENERATIONS

Somewhere a shop of hanging meats,
shop of stink and blood, block and cleaver;

somewhere an immigrant, grandfather, stranger
with my last name. That man

untying his apron in 1910, scrubbing off
the pale fat, going home past brownstones

and churches, past vendors, streetcars, arias,
past the clatter of supper dishes, going home

to his new son, my father—
What is he to me, butcher with sausage fingers,

old Italian leaning over a child somewhere
in New York City, somewhere alive, what is he

that I go back to look for him, years after his death
and my father's death, knowing only

a name, a few scraps my father fed me?
My father who shortened that name, who hacked off

three lovely syllables, who raised American children.
What is the past to me

that I have to go back, pronouncing that word
in the silence of a cemetery, what is this stone

coming apart in my hands like bread, name
I eat and expel? Somewhere the smell of figs

and brine, strung garlic, rosemary and olives;
somewhere that place. Somewhere a boat

rocking, crossing over, entering the harbor. I wait
on the dock, one face in a crowd of faces.

Families disembark and stream toward the city,
and though I walk among them for hours,

hungry, haunting the streets,
I can't tell which of them is mine.

Somewhere a steak is wrapped in thick paper,
somewhere my grandmother is laid in the earth,

and my young father shines shoes on a corner,
turning his back to the Old World, forgetting.

I walk the night city, looking up at lit windows,
and there is no table set for me, nowhere

I can go to be filled. This is the city
of grandparents, immigrants, arrivals,

where I've come too late with my name,
an empty plate. This is the place.

2.

Blue Door

NEAR HERON LAKE

During the night, horses passed close
to our parked van. Inside I woke cold
under the sleeping bag, hearing their heavy sway,
the gravel harsh under their hooves as they moved off
down the bank to the river. You slept on,
though maybe in your dream you felt them enter
our life just long enough to cause that slight
stirring, a small spasm in your limbs and then
a sigh so quiet, so close to being nothing
but the next breath, I could believe you never guessed
how those huge animals broke out of the dark and came
toward us. Or how afraid I was before I understood
what they were—only horses, not anything
that would hurt us. The next morning
I watched you at the edge of the river
washing your face, your bare chest beaded with bright water,
and knew how much we needed this,
the day ahead with its calm lake
we would swim in, naked, able to touch again.
You were so beautiful. And I thought
the marriage might never end.

CRAFTS FAIR, PICURIS PUEBLO

Bent over a black pot on an outdoor stove
a woman lifts fry bread
dripping from the oil with a stick and calls

for more Cokes from the house.
We drift among the booths
where families sit with quilts

and pots, carved turtles and tiny katsinas.
The sky's white, the heat like cotton batting.
A lone carnival ride revolves,

empty cars bolted to a steel rod.
Whatever we came for, it isn't this sad, dusty field
or the trays of turquoise rings and bracelets,

the same we've seen in every trading post
along the way. Why not admit
there's no place our love will be easy again,

however far we drive into the mountains;
why not say it here, where the air
is heavy with flies, where nothing is trying

very hard to be graceful
or even kind. But maybe it is kindness, after all,
that keeps us from talking; we walk side by side,

tear the soft bread in two and share it.
Up the hill are the private houses of the pueblo.
At the half-built church

you stop to snap a picture
of the finished arch, the piled adobe bricks,
a place our friends will later take for ruins.

COLLAPSING POEM

The woman stands on the front steps, sobbing.
The man stays just inside the house,
leaning against the doorjamb. It's late, a wet
fog has left a sheer film over the windows
of cars along the street. The woman is drunk.
She begs the man, but he won't let her in.
Say it matters what happened between them;
say you can't judge whose fault this all is,
given the lack of context, given your own failures
with those you meant most to love.
Or maybe you don't care about them yet.
Maybe you need some way
to put yourself in this scene, some minor detail
that will make them seem so real you try to enter
this page to keep them from doing
to each other what you've done to someone,
somewhere: think about that for a minute,
while she keeps crying, and he speaks
in a voice so measured and calm he might be
talking to a child frightened by something
perfectly usual: darkness, thunder,
the coldness of the human heart.
But she's not listening, because now
she's hitting him, beating her fists against the chest
she laid her head on so many nights.
And by now, if you've been moved, it's because
you're thinking with regret of the person
this poem set out to remind you of,
and what you want more than anything is what
the man in the poem wants: for her to shut up.
And if you could only drive down that street
and emerge from the fog, maybe you
could get her to stop, but I can't do it.
All I can do is stand at that open door
making things worse. That's my talent,

that's why this poem won't get finished unless
you drag me from it, away from that man;
for Christ's sake, hurry, just pull up and keep
the motor running and take me wherever you're going.

THE DIVORCÉE AND GIN

I love the frosted pints you come in,
and the tall bottles with their uniformed men;
the bars where you're poured chilled
into shallow glasses, the taste of drowned olives,
and the scrawled benches where I see you
passed impatiently from one mouth
to another, the bag twisted tight around
your neck, the hand that holds you
shaking a little from its need
which is the true source of desire; God, I love
what you do to me at night when we're alone,
how you wait for me to take you into me
until I'm so confused with you I can't
stand up anymore. I know you want me
helpless, each cell whimpering, and I give
you that, letting you have me just the way
you like it. And when you're finished
you turn your face to the wall while I curl
around you again, and enter another morning
with aspirin and the useless ache
that comes from loving, too well,
those who, under the guise of pleasure,
destroy everything they touch.

AT MOSS BEACH

At night along this coast the boats
slipped to shore with their illegal cargo.
The long cars waited, lights hushed,
for the liquor to be hauled up the cliff.
We've stopped at the edge of it this morning,
held by the lush purple spread of ice plant
in the hollows below. Whoever was here then
could not have imagined our lives, just as I
can't imagine the face of some new lover
after we're over. But the past opens so easily:
the stars sink, the prow cleaves dense fog,
the sleek unseen shapes of the limousines are humming
somewhere ahead, and behind the boat
the white froth of the wake travels
over the churning water. Packed in roped crates
are the bottles, in each one the rattle
of dice thrown down, a man loosened from
his money, a woman in a blue dress leaning
against him, the thrilling surf of her laughter.
Gliding through the dark, can the crew hear
our voices? You pull one vivid flower from its home
in the earth. I tell you it will always
make me think of you, this startling
brush stroke that repeats itself for miles
along the shore, this particular water
that today holds a freighter heading out,
a lone crow arrowing after it.

RANCHOS DE TAOS, AUGUST

I'm alone all day.
In the afternoon, thunder.
The birds' cries become more numerous,
like first drops of rain,
and I go outside to look at the mountains.
No one knows I do this—
not the man I miss,
not the friends who will return this evening.
All around their house the sky
stitches together the loose scraps of dark.
I feel small, and purposeless;
even the ant, rust-colored, dragging the torn
wing of a dragonfly across my shadow
and into the sagebrush, has more to do.
I tell my heart
to be patient, that joy returns,
but it doesn't want to listen.
It wants to tell me
that the storm comes toward us,
heavy with each named grief,
and slams all the windows
in the empty house.

BLUE DOOR

Today I passed the house
we rented last summer.
It was only a glimpse
as I drove by—
blue door,
adobe arch painted with flowers.
In memory
your dusty van is parked on the gravel
and you're standing at the stove
while I curl
on the couch with a book,
pretending to read,
but secretly
watching you, loving
how you look—
intent on our meal,
on getting it right.
How clearly
I can see everything:
cars passing
on the road outside,
you, shirtless, leaning over
a cast-iron pot,
me holding a few useless
words in my hands.
Nothing I'll say
will make you stay with me,
nothing erase how you'll turn
toward me, offering the wooden spoon
so that I get up,
and come to you, and taste
that salt on my tongue.

3.

Last Call

INTIMACY

The woman in the café making my cappuccino—dark eyes, dyed
    red hair,
sleeveless black turtleneck—used to be lovers with the man I'm
    seeing now.
She doesn't know me; we're strangers, but still I can't glance at her
casually, as I used to, before I knew. She stands at the machine,
    sinking the nozzle
into a froth of milk, staring at nothing—I don't know what she's
    thinking.
For all I know she might be remembering my lover, remembering
    whatever happened
between them—he's never told me, except to say that it wasn't
    important, and then
he changed the subject quickly, too quickly now that I think about
    it; might he,
after all, have been lying, didn't an expression of pain cross his
    face for just
an instant? I can't be sure. And really it was nothing, I tell myself;
there's no reason for me to feel awkward standing here, or
    complicitous,
as though there's something significant between us.
She could be thinking of anything; why, now, do I have the sudden
    suspicion
that she knows, that she feels me studying her, trying to imagine
    them together?—
her lipstick's dark red, darker than her hair—trying to see him
    kissing her, turning her over in bed
the way he likes to have me. I wonder if maybe
there were things about her he preferred, things he misses now
    that we're together;
sometimes, when he and I are making love, there are moments
I'm overwhelmed by sadness, and though I'm there with him I
    can't help thinking
of my ex-husband's hands, which I especially loved, and I want to
    go back

to that old intimacy, which often felt like the purest happiness
I'd ever known, or would. But all that's over; and besides, weren't
   there other lovers
who left no trace? When I see them now, I can barely remember
what they looked like undressed, or how it felt to have them
inside me. So what is it I feel as she pours the black espresso into
   the milk,
and pushes the cup toward me, and I give her the money,
and our eyes meet for just a second, and our fingers touch?

THE EMBERS

My friend Priscilla and I used to stop in for drinks, after I'd taught
    my wretched poetry class—
most of the students were lithium-dosed, or alcoholic, sprung for
    the evening from cheap rooms
in the seedier part of downtown, living on state checks, nourished
    by a belief in their latent genius,
which they were sure I would discover. They were desperate to
    publish, though criminally indifferent
to actual poetry. After class, the Embers restored my faith in the
    kind of failure that is sufficient
unto itself, without requiring the amplifications of art. There was
    always a guy who could barely speak
slumped over the bar, always a boozed-up old crone, and usually
    some ill-at-ease young couple
who'd wandered in from the street of respectable cafés and pricey
    boutiques. Once, Priscilla danced
on the bar, but on her knees, because the ceiling was low. Always a
    song about lost love throbbing
on the jukebox, always those wooden doors with the high
    windows like portholes, sealing in
the damp smell of cigarettes and defeat. Did I say always? One
    night I passed by there,
after weeks away from the neighborhood, and there was nothing
    left. The new place was all plate glass,
and blue neon blared PLUTO'S, and it was just as though I'd
    stepped into space: here's where
the bar was, here's the bathroom where I once stood up, dizzy,
    wiped my face with a wet paper towel
and staggered back out. Here are the ashes of that night, and all
    my attempts to teach anyone
how to do anything but stay upright, and keep going, while you're
    feeling so sick you can hardly breathe.

LAST CALL

It's the hour when everyone's drunk
and the bar turns marvelous, music
swirling over the red booths,
smoke rising from neglected cigarettes as in each glass
ice slides into other ice, dissolving;
it's when one stranger nudges another
and says, staring at the blurred rows of pour spouts,
I hear they banned dwarf tossing in France,
and the second man nods
and lays his head on the bar's slick surface,
not caring if he dies there, wanting, in fact, to die there
among the good friends he's just met, his cheek
in a wet pool of spilled beer.
It's when the woman in the corner gets up
and wobbles to the middle of the room,
leaving her blouse draped over a stool. Someone is buying
the house a final round, the cabs are being summoned,
and the gods that try to save us from ourselves
are taking us by the neck, gently,
and dropping us into the night; it's the hour
of the blind, and the dead, of lost loves
who come to claim you, finally, holding open
the swinging door, repeating over and over
a name that must be yours.

NOTHING

There's a riddle my daughter tells,
I don't remember all of it, but the end
goes like this: *Dead people eat it,*
but if you eat it, you die.
The answer is *nothing*, she says,
and tells the whole thing over, saying *nothing*
until it's something—food of the dead,
heaping plates of nothing set out before
the graves, detergent stains on the butter knives,
the shallow spoons, the tiny, special forks
for prying out the smallest shreds
of nothing, nothing ladled into urns
to float the ashes, the blue bits of bone,
hot steamy nothing sloshing over the tureen
no one carries across the cropped grass,
glossy substance the dead devour until
they're sick and groaning, toxic nothing
the living die from,
nothing in the fridge, in the house,
nothing that satisfies this hunger;
so eat.

LAST GIFTS

for Al

They were gathered in the room next to the kitchen, where he had his hospital bed cranked up. A writer he had published brought him a long red boa and draped it around his neck; he looked like someone drowning, a small head floating on feathery waves. Someone else brought a pillow stitched with a picture of Elvis, with the words "King of Rock and Roll" across the top. There were red splotches on his arms, and his hand shook slightly when he poured water into the glass on his tray. A poet took a book off the crowded shelves, sat on the edge of the bed and read to him for a while. Someone accidentally stood on the oxygen hose; no one noticed until he began to cough, and there was some consternation, and then relieved laughter and joking. The party grew more animated; people refilled their drinks, and everyone started talking at once. His wife went to the kitchen and brought back a big silver bowl of buttered popcorn and passed it around. For a few moments it seemed as though they had forgotten him. Then someone finished a story, someone else paused to think of the right word, and a silence opened and spread through the brightly lit room. The guests looked at one another; some had tears in their eyes. They turned to the bed, where the sick man sat smiling at them in his red boa, and he knew this was what it would be like when he was gone. And then he was.

THE REVERED POET INSTRUCTS
HER STUDENTS ON THE IMPORTANCE
OF REVISION

Listen. I'm trying to tell you
how easily the poem you thought
was a beautiful woman becomes
cronelike by a kind of witchery.

How easy, you thought, to write a poem:
you scrawled last night in your journal
and in the morning, by a kind of witchery,
the poem was born, perfect, immortal.

But soon, too soon, what you scrawled in your journal
begins moaning, pitches forward and wails, hating
itself, the fact it was ever born—imperfect, mortal
and suffering the way everything suffers,

every moaning lover, every wailing child,
each creature destined to be isolate and alone
and suffering the way everything suffers,
but I said that, didn't I, I explained already about suffering

and about each one of you, destined to be isolate and alone
because writing is lonely work, is what I'm trying to say,
did I say that, did I explain already? I'm suffering
through your poems, and my own, oh God I feel

so desperately lonely is what I'm trying to say,
look at you you're so young all of you,
I don't care about your poems, or my own,
do you know how fast it goes, all I want is to be

as young as all of you, look at you
you're so fucking clueless, oh I want
my life back, where did it go, I want it all to be
different but I'm standing here, lecturing again—

on what, on what? Oh fuck it,
listen, I was a beautiful woman,
you think I want to be standing here, *lecturing*? Look again.
Listen. I'm trying to tell you.

PHANTOM ANNIVERSARY

Imagine the marriage lasting,
the lilies blooming in the black vase
for years, the water still fresh.
The man and woman are looking at each other
as they fuck, blooming and looking,
and the angels are looking, too,
opening their beautiful abstract mouths
as though they are about to say something
neither difficult nor true.
The man and woman are oblivious.
They grow fainter and fainter without caring.
And the angels fold their wings flat
and plummet toward them like stones.

FOR SLEEP

My daughter's terrified of spiders; at night she worries
they'll crawl over her while she's sleeping, and sometimes when
    she's sleeping

she dreams they do, and wakes up and runs to my bed,
crying while I try to soothe her. I tell her

how they're sacred to some Indian tribes, I take her outside
where one has strung a glistening web under a beam

in the narrow walkway between our house and the next,
a sight she actually does find beautiful—but the spider,

hanging there, swaying a little in the breeze,
she cringes from. I take down a book to show her drawings:

crab spider, orb-weaver, wolf spider dragging her egg sac
into the long grass. I teach her *spinnerets*,

those makers of silk. But soon she knows *tarantula, black widow*,
the suffocated housefly bundled in white threads.

She understands the poison, the devouring mate,
how love is less than the slimmest spun strand.

She wakes up alone, can feel the tiny legs ticking across her cheek,
the small malevolence that seeks her out; again

she runs to my bed, and burrows in beside me,
and I hold her until she quiets, and we wait together for sleep.

THE PROMISE

When my daughter confessed she'd wanted to end her life at ten—
stepped out on the window ledge and stood there, at the edge

of a decision—we promised never to kill ourselves, never
to abandon each other. And I've never told her about the night

two years later when I came to a place in myself
where it seemed, for the first time, possible—

the way a door appears suddenly in a fairy tale, where the wall
    was solid.
I knew I could do it—I was drinking

and heartsick, I had enough pills.
I sat on my bed, arms around my knees,

and rocked the way I used to as a child.
Then, I'd believed in God; I would talk to Him

half the night sometimes, knowing
He was there, in heaven, just above the ceiling of my parents'
    room.

But now there was no one. Only
a couple of cats, locked together in some yard or alley, yowling

until someone raised a window, yelled and slammed it shut.
What a mess I was. How fiercely I loved her.

᪣

THE BODY IN EXTREMIS

First I think of it as a factory
where the foreman's passed out drunk
in his high room with the little window
while the radio slides into static
and down below no one gives a shit
about pride in labor considering what they're paid
so one by one they're taking off
their goggles and aprons and building a huge
bonfire in the center of the room and banging
the metal carts against one another while a few
holdouts stay grimly at their tasks
and try to ignore the din. But all that's
mechanical and wrong so I close my eyes
to try again: your body is a vase of flowers,
their brown stalks slick in the fetid water,
the shrunken tissue of the petals falling
on a scarred table beside an old couch—
stained, burn-holed—a sunken shape in a darkened
living room. Outside is the worst
section of the city, figures hurrying into doorways,
up to no good, random gunshots and exploding glass,
alarms, alarms—amazing what the mind can do
and still fail to absorb the plain fact
of you, railed-in and dying.
In this nearly sterile room
there are no more ways to imagine
your thin form beneath the covers, your face
I now bend close to kiss,
and whatever I make of the grief
that's coming, it won't change this, *this*.

RAIN

is what I can't bear going on & not
easing all day hitting the windows like someone
throwing shovelfuls of dirt onto a
coffin keeping me in bed sick but not physically only
reading a poet's lines about Vietnam thinking of
Harry & Danny & Ron how long ago it was now
I don't know them or only my body remembers
lying beneath Harry on the hard
ground of the field frozen with little stars
of frost his hands holding an M16 or a woman
with black hair or my shoulders as he
came inside me crying & Danny strapping on
his wooden leg to teach me karate saying *Don't
be afraid to maim* his naked thigh scarred
& oddly beautiful & his one foot the divot of flesh gouged
out or Ron talking bitterly about America & the night
I pushed his wheelchair too fast ran it
off the sidewalk into a tree & we laughed &
how I'd grow so tired of listening to him & never
knowing if he cared what I thought all of it
gone into my history of loss a litany I need
to sing I don't know why today it's just the rain
keeps up & I feel so cold inside I can't get out
of bed or understand why these ghosts
of men come back to press me down I couldn't
help them or I did maybe a little tenderness a
breast or kiss what I could offer not knowing I was
so young believing I could heal them the rain
relentless against the windows when will it stop oh when

BEGINNING WITH HIS BODY AND ENDING
IN A SMALL TOWN

It's true I can't forget any part of him,
not the long vein rising up along the underside of his cock,
or the brushy hair around his balls, dank star of the asshole,
high arches of his feet, strawberry mole on his left cheek—
imperfection that made his face exquisite—
and the freckles scattered over his back,
white insides of his wrists, I remember those too,
and the scar on his belly oh I'm kissing it now,
he belongs to me so purely now he's left me,
he'll never come back, his face as he lets go inside me,
I'll never see it again, I stand dripping
in the shower where I once knelt
before him to drink whatever came
out of him, sometimes he would watch
me as I walked naked around the room,
here I am, it's the same room, I'm still
seeing his face the night it closed
to me forever like a failed business, iron grillwork
across the door, dirty windows, trash scattered
over the floor and the fixtures taken out, I turned
away and stumbled down the street, the one bar
was open, the saddest bar in the world, filled
with painted clowns and a few drunks, the owner had passed out
in a booth, covered by his coat, his girlfriend was working
and said *The usual, right?* and I couldn't say a word
except *Please*, and I took a stool and drank
what she served and served and served.

TELL ME

I am going to stop thinking about my losses now
and listen to yours. I'm so sick of dragging them

with me wherever I go, like children up too late
who should be curled in their own beds

under the only blanket that warms them.
I am going to send them home while I stay

at this party all night with the loud music pumping
and the dancers moving gracelessly under the lights

and the drinkers spilling their scotches on their sleeves.
I am going to join them. I'm going to drink until

I'm so wasted I forget I have children, I'll dance
until I ache, until I make a spectacle of myself.

So tell me. Tell me how you hurt
even though I can't help you. Tell me

their ages, how they keep you up nights,
how sometimes you wish they were dead

but keep finding yourself gazing at them
tenderly while they sleep. Then, please, dance with me,

hold me while we fool ourselves
they aren't out there, pressing their damp

hollow faces to the windows. Tell me
that if we kiss a new one won't start to slip

from each of us, tell me you can't already feel
the little hole burning in your side

or hear the others moving over to make room,
shrieking and clapping with joy.

MERMAID SONG

for Aya at fifteen

Damp-haired from the bath, you drape yourself
upside down across the sofa, reading,
one hand idly sunk into a bowl
of crackers, goldfish with smiles stamped on.
I think they are growing gills, swimming
up the sweet air to reach you. Small girl,
my slim miracle, they multiply.
In the black hours when I lie sleepless,
near drowning, dread-heavy, your face
is the bright lure I look for, love's hook
piercing me, hauling me cleanly up.

SPILL

You turn away. I remember again
the first time you turned toward me,
knocking over your glass.
We sat at a table, getting drunk.

The first time you turned toward me
I knew this moment would come:
two people getting drunk at a table,
getting it over with. And though

I knew this moment would come
I couldn't help kissing you,
getting it over with, although
we might have stayed friends, otherwise;

but I couldn't help kissing you,
starting things up—the hasty undressing, the love
we might have kept as friends, if we were wise.
Now, stupidly, we've come to the end.

Starting things up was hasty, love.
Knocking over your glass
I stare stupidly. We've come to the end.
You turn away. I remember again.

THE LOVERS

*Thus the physical event and the content of the human
mind were inseparable.*
      —Harold J. Morowitz, "Rediscovering the Mind"

What do they want from each other,
that man and woman clinging together and staggering
around the kitchen, the man's tongue completely
inside her mouth, her breasts flattened against
his chest, what is it they can't seem to

get to, why do they look to me like two
people roped together and thrown overboard,
sinking and thrashing in the stove's light?
What makes them seem so desperate
when they're only kissing, really only

a memory of kissing; why do I think of them and feel
my lungs burning, my heart filling with water?
I want them to break free of each other and reach
the surface again, or else I want them
to hurry up, I want them to drown. But they go on

and on until I'm exhausted, until I lie down
and finally stop caring. I'm sealing them into a box
like in that paradox the scientist proposed—
Schrödinger's cat, that as long as you don't look
might be alive or dead. I'm putting them in there

with the imaginary jar of poison,
the hypothetical hammer, with their letters
and little gifts, the photographs that say
they're happy, and I'm not going to look anymore,
I'm not going to kill them or save them.

❧

AFFAIR

God it's sexual, opening a beer when you swore you wouldn't
    drink tonight,
taking the first deep gulp, the foam backing up in the long amber
    neck

of the Pacifico bottle as you set it on the counter, the head spilling
    over
so you bend to fit your mouth against the cold lip

and drink, because what you are, aren't you, is a drinker—maybe
    not a lush,
not an alcoholic, not yet anyway, but don't you want

a glass of something most nights, don't you need the gesture
of reaching for it, raising it high and swallowing down and
    savoring

the sweetness, or the scalding, knowing you're going to give
    yourself to it
like a lover, whether or not he fills up the leaky balloon of your
    heart—

don't you believe in trying to fill it, no matter what the odds,
don't you believe it still might happen, aren't you that kind of
    woman?

❧

4.

Good Girl

ONSET

Watching that frenzy of insects above the bush of white flowers,
bush I see everywhere on hill after hill, all I can think of
is how terrifying spring is, in its tireless, mindless replications.
Everywhere emergence: seed case, chrysalis, uterus, endless
    manufacturing.
And the wrapped stacks of Styrofoam cups in the grocery, lately
I can't stand them, the shelves of canned beans and soups, freezers
of identical dinners; then the snowflake-diamond-snowflake of the
    rug
beneath my chair, rows of books turning their backs,
even my two feet, how they mirror each other oppresses me,
the way they fit so perfectly together, how I can nestle one big toe
    into the other
like little continents that have drifted; my God the unity of
    everything,
my hands and eyes, yours; doesn't that frighten you sometimes,
    remembering
the pleasure of nakedness in fresh sheets, all the lovers there before
    you,
beside you, crowding you out? And the scouring griefs,
don't look at them all or they'll kill you, you can barely encompass
    your own;
I'm saying I know all about you, whoever you are, it's spring
and it's starting again, the longing that begins, and begins, and
    begins.

"WHAT DO WOMEN WANT?"

I want a red dress.
I want it flimsy and cheap,
I want it too tight, I want to wear it
until someone tears it off me.
I want it sleeveless and backless,
this dress, so no one has to guess
what's underneath. I want to walk down
the street past Thrifty's and the hardware store
with all those keys glittering in the window,
past Mr. and Mrs. Wong selling day-old
donuts in their café, past the Guerra brothers
slinging pigs from the truck and onto the dolly,
hoisting the slick snouts over their shoulders.
I want to walk like I'm the only
woman on earth and I can have my pick.
I want that red dress bad.
I want it to confirm
your worst fears about me,
to show you how little I care about you
or anything except what
I want. When I find it, I'll pull that garment
from its hanger like I'm choosing a body
to carry me into this world, through
the birth-cries and the love-cries too,
and I'll wear it like bones, like skin,
it'll be the goddamned
dress they bury me in.

GOOD GIRL

Look at you, sitting there being good.
After two years you're still dying for a cigarette.
And not drinking on weekdays, who thought that one up?
Don't you want to run to the corner right now
for a fifth of vodka and have it with cranberry juice
and a nice lemon slice, wouldn't the backyard
that you're so sick of staring out into
look better then, the tidy yard your landlord tends
day and night—the fence with its fresh coat of paint,
the ash-free barbecue, the patio swept clean of small twigs—
don't you want to mess it all up, to roll around
like a dog in his flower beds? Aren't you a dog anyway,
always groveling for love and begging to be petted?
You ought to get into the garbage and lick the insides
of the can, the greasy wrappers, the picked-over bones;
you ought to drive your snout into the coffee grounds.
Ah, coffee! Why not gulp some down with four cigarettes
and then blast naked into the streets, and leap on the first
beautiful man you find? The words *Ruin me*, haven't they
been jailed in your throat for forty years, isn't it time
you set them loose in slutty dresses and torn fishnets
to totter around in five-inch heels and smeared mascara?
Sure it's time. You've rolled over long enough.
Forty, forty-one. At the end of all this
there's one lousy biscuit, and it tastes like dirt.
So get going. Listen, they're howling for you now:
up and down the block your neighbors' dogs
burst into frenzied barking and won't shut up.

PHYSICS

In the darkness of the booth, you have to find
the slot blindly and fumble the quarter in. The black
shade goes up. Now there's a naked woman

dancing before you and you're looking
at her knees, then raising your eyes
to the patch of wiry hair which she obligingly parts

with two fingers while her other hand
palms her body from breast to hip
and it's you doing it, for a second

you're touching her like that and when
you lift your face to hers she's not
gazing into space as you expected but

looking back, right at you, with an expression
that says *I love you, I belong to you compl—*
but then the barrier descends. You shove

another quarter in, but the thing has to close down,
before slowly opening again like a pupil adjusting
to the absence of light and by the time it does

you've lost her. She's moved on to the next
low window holding someone's blurred face,
and another woman is coming nearer

under the stage lights and in the mirrors,
looking so happy to see you trapped there
like some poor fish in a plastic baggie

that will finally be released into a small bowl
with a ceramic castle and a few colored rocks,
and you open your mouth just like a fish waiting

for the flakes of food, understanding nothing
of what causes them to rain down
upon you. You can feel your hunger sharpening

as she thrusts herself over and over into
the air between you. And now, unbelievably,
there comes into your mind

not the image of fucking her
but an explanation you heard once
of what vast distances exist

between any two electrons. Suppose,
the scientist said, the atom were the size
of an orange; then imagine that orange as big

as the earth. The electrons inside it
would be only the size of cherries. *Cherries,*
you think, and inserting your quarter you see one

sitting on an ice floe in the Antarctic, a pinprick
of blood, and another in a village in Northern Africa
being rolled on the tongue of a dusty child

while the dancer shakes her breasts at you,
displaying nipples you know you'll never
bite into in this lifetime; all you can do

is hold tight to the last useless coins
and repeat to yourself that they're solid,
they're definitely solid, you can definitely feel them.

ALIENS

Now that you're finally happy
you notice how sad your friends are.
One calls you from a pay phone, crying.
Her husband has cancer; only a few months,
maybe less, before his body gives in.
She's tired all the time, can barely eat.
What can you say that will help her?
You yourself are ravenous.
You come so intensely with your new lover
you wonder if you've turned
into someone else. Maybe an alien
has taken over your body
in order to experience the good life
here on earth: dark rum and grapefruit juice,
fucking on the kitchen floor,
then showering together and going out
to eat and eat. When your friends call—
the woman drinking too much, the one who lost
her brother, the ex-lover whose right ear
went dead and then began buzzing—
the alien doesn't want to listen.
More food, it whines. *Fuck me again*,
it whispers, *and afterward we'll go to the circus*.
The phone rings. *Don't answer it*.
You reach for a fat éclair,
bite into it while the room fills
with aliens—wandering, star-riddled creatures
who vibrate in the rapturous air,
longing to come down and join you,
looking for a place they can rest.

LIKE THAT

Love me like a wrong turn on a bad road late at night, with no
    moon and no town anywhere
and a large hungry animal moving heavily through the brush in
    the ditch.
Love me with a blindfold over your eyes and the sound of rusty
    water
blurting from the faucet in the kitchen, leaking down through
the floorboards to hot cement. Do it without asking,
without wondering or thinking anything, while the machinery's
shut down and the watchman's slumped asleep before his small TV
showing the empty garage, the deserted hallways, while the thieves
    slice through
the fence with steel clippers. Love me when you can't find
a decent restaurant open anywhere, when you're alone in a glaring
    diner
with two nuns arguing in the back booth, when your eggs are
    greasy
and your hash browns underdone. Snick the buttons off the front
    of my dress
and toss them one by one into the pond where carp lurk just
    beneath the surface,
their cold fins waving. Love me on the hood of a truck no one's
    driven
in years, sunk to its fenders in weeds and dead sunflowers;
and in the lilies, your mouth on my white throat, while turtles
    drag
their bellies through slick mud, through the footprints of coots and
    ducks.
Do it when no one's looking, when the riots begin and the planes
    open up,
when the bus leaps the curb and the driver hits the brakes and the
    pedal sinks to the floor,
while someone hurls a plate against the wall and picks up another,
love me like a freezing shot of vodka, like pure agave, love me

when you're lonely, when we're both too tired to speak, when you
    don't believe
in anything, listen, there isn't anything, it doesn't matter; lie down
with me and close your eyes, the road curves here, I'm cranking up
    the radio
and we're going, we won't turn back as long as you love me,
as long as you keep on doing it exactly like that.

PRAYER

Sometimes, when we're lying after love,
I look at you and see your body's future
of lying beneath the earth; putting the heel
of my hand against your rib I feel how faint
and far away the heartbeat is. I rest
my cheek against your left nipple and listen
to the surge of blood, seeing your life splashed out,
filmy water hurled from a pot
onto dry grass. And I want to be pressed
deep into the bed and covered over,
the way a seed is pressed into a hole,
the dirt tamped down with a trowel.
I want to be a failed seed, the kind
that doesn't grow, that doesn't know it's meant to.
I want to lie here without moving, lifeless
as an animal that's slaughtered, its blood smeared
on a doorpost, I want death to take me if it
has to, to spare you, I want it to pass over.

FINE

You're lucky. It's always them and not you. The family trapped in the fire, the secretary slain in the parking lot holding her coffee and Egg McMuffin, the ones rushed to emergency after the potluck. You're lucky you didn't touch the tuna casserole, and went for the baked chicken instead. Your friend with breast cancer that was detected too late—metastasized to the lymph nodes, the lungs, a few months to live—lucky there's no history in your family. Another friend's fiancé, heart attack at forty-seven. You lie in bed at night, your head on your lover's chest, and you're grateful. Your teenaged daughter, unlike all her friends, hasn't become sullen or combative, addicted to cigarettes or booze. She's not in the bathroom with her finger down her throat to throw up dinner. You and your family are fine. You're happy. It's like you're in your own little boat, just you, sailing along, and the wind is up and nothing's leaking. All around you you can see other boats filling up, flipping over, sliding under. If you look into the water you can watch them for a while, going down slowly, getting smaller and farther away. Soon, if nothing happens to you, if your luck holds, really holds, you'll end up completely alone.

THE WITNESS

She sees how he ruins his own beauty,
how he craves the gold pour of rum into the glass
with its single cube of ice, its splash of red juice,
how the threadlike veins rise to the surface of his cheeks
the way carp in a pond come up for bread.
Each night he empties a pack of cigarettes
at the kitchen window, taking the smoke
deep into his tarnished lungs where the sputum
is already forming, waiting to be hawked up in the sink,
smoke billowing in his blood, the sticky platelets thickening.
It is the one thing in his life he has perfected—
this ease of crumpling a soiled filter into an ashtray,
turning his fine profile to her as he lifts
his drink, his reflection in the window's black rectangle
floating above the lights of neighboring houses.
She feels helpless to keep him from anything,
the way a child is helpless among the adults
who determine its fate; she sees she's only here
as a witness, someone who will remember
each detail with perfect clarity
after the worst is over,
after it's too late to save anyone.

LEAVING SONG

Good-bye to how you'd curl away in sleep,
one hand to your forehead, doing the hard work
of dreaming; and to the early dark,
you on the bed's edge, pulling on your shoes,
the quick kiss before you joined the others
sealed into cars along the highway,
going away all day and coming back
to set the paper bag beside the sink
and pour the first drink, and the next, the ones
after that; good-bye to your drunkenness,
which I admit I liked because of how
you'd cry sometimes, or follow me from room
to room, naked, dripping from a bath,
able to say what you couldn't, sober.
Love, I'm going. Line up the drained bottles,
audience for your beloved Schumann
pounded out at the piano, the rhythms awkward,
the wrong notes repeating... Good-bye, this
is the leaving song, it's almost over.
I used to lie awake and hold you as you slept;
when you snored I smoothed the fine hair
on your head, and watched your lovely face
and wished you someone else, who even
in the lamplight, and the smoke-thick air
from your constant cigarettes, never would appear.

ONE-NIGHT STANDS

Those men I fucked when I was drunk,
I can't even see their faces anymore.
Or the shape of their hands, hard
bones of their hips knocking against me,
curve of an ass or shoulder. Whatever
I tasted as they slid over me, nameless,
whatever words they tongued into me,
I don't have them. What I have
are the bars I met them in, the sweat
on a glass of beer, the dense granules of red
or blue light sifting toward me, sharp swell
of music and a voice saying *Let's get out
of here*. We always went to a place
I'd never be able to find again
if I ever bothered to look.
There are people we're meant
to lose, moments that rinse off.
And there are still nights I lie awake
with the pulse, the throb,
that says *Let's go*
somewhere and watch the moon rise
over three rows of bottles and a cash register.
Let someone else pay. Ask for a cigarette
and the fire to light it, burn a few hours,
show me you love me that much.

GETTING OLDER

Sometimes what you remember is their voices again,
coming on inside you like strung lights in your blood,
certain words they'd tongue differently
from anyone else, or your own name
and its surprisingly infinite nuances.
And sometimes you remember their hands,
not touching you but draped over a steering wheel
or cupped briefly around a cigarette,
anywhere you could watch them
in their life apart from you, knowing how
they'd find you later, blind but sure,
and come to rest where you needed them.
You remember the hardness of their bellies,
the soft line of hair that swirls down
toward the cock, the look of each one
that entered you and then withdrew, or lay
quietly inside awhile longer before slipping
away like a girl sneaking out in the middle
of the night, high heels dangling from one hand
as her stockinged feet drew sparks from the rug.
Sometimes you wander the house all day,
the fog outside stalled at the tops
of trees, refusing to rise higher and reveal
the world you hope is still there, the one
in which you're still a woman
some beautiful man might helplessly
move toward. And you remember how one
looked at you the first time you undressed,
how another didn't mind that you cried.
Sometimes it's enough just to say
their names like a rosary, ordinary names
linked by nothing but the fact
that they belong to men who loved you. And finally
you depend on that, you pray it's enough
to last, if it has to, the rest of your life.

FOR DESIRE

Give me the strongest cheese, the one that stinks best;
and I want the good wine, the swirl in crystal
surrendering the bruised scent of blackberries,
or cherries, the rich spurt in the back
of the throat, the holding it there before swallowing.
Give me the lover who yanks open the door
of his house and presses me to the wall
in the dim hallway, and keeps me there until I'm drenched
and shaking, whose kisses arrive by the boatload
and begin their delicious diaspora
through the cities and small towns of my body.
To hell with the saints, with the martyrs
of my childhood meant to instruct me
in the power of endurance and faith,
to hell with the next world and its pallid angels
swooning and sighing like Victorian girls.
I want this world. I want to walk into
the ocean and feel it trying to drag me along
like I'm nothing but a broken bit of scratched glass,
and I want to resist it. I want to go
staggering and flailing my way
through the bars and back rooms,
through the gleaming hotels and the weedy
lots of abandoned sunflowers and the parks
where dogs are let off their leashes
in spite of the signs, where they sniff each
other and roll together in the grass, I want to
lie down somewhere and suffer for love until
it nearly kills me, and then I want to get up again
and put on that little black dress and wait
for you, yes you, to come over here
and get down on your knees and tell me
just how fucking good I look.

FLOOD

How images enter you, the shutter of the body
clicking when you're not even looking:
smooth chill of satin sheets, piano keys, a pastry's glazy crust
floating up, suddenly, so the hairs along your arm
lift in that current of memory, and your tongue tastes
the sweet salt of a lover as he surges
against you, plunges toward the place you can't
dive into but which is deepening each moment
you are alive, the black pupil widening,
the man going down and in, the food and
champagne and music and light, there is no bottom to this,
silt and murk of losses that won't ever settle,
and the huge unsleeping fish, voracious for pleasure,
and the soundless fathoms where nothing
yet exists, this minute, the next, the last
breath let out and not returning, oh hold
on to me as the waters rise, don't be afraid,
we are going to join the others, we are going
to remember and tell them everything.

ACKNOWLEDGMENTS

Grateful acknowledgment is made to the editors of the following publications in which these works or earlier versions of them previously appeared:

Alaska Quarterly Review: "Aliens," "Flood," "Like That," "Mermaid Song," "Salmon," "Target," "Tell Me";

Amaranth: "Siamese";

American Poetry Review: "Phantom Anniversary," "Physics";

Another Chicago Magazine: "Beginning with His Body and Ending in a Small Town," "Rain," "'What Do Women Want?'";

Bakunin: "Crafts Fair, Picuris Pueblo";

Barrow Street: "The Promise," "Virgin Spring";

Bastard Review: "Therapy";

Chelsea: "Generations," "Night of the Living, Night of the Dead," "One-Night Stands," "Onset" (as "Likeness"), "The Revered Poet Instructs Her Students on the Importance of Revision";

Columbia: "Prayer";

Five Points: "For Desire," "The Lovers," "The Moment";

Fourteen Hills: "Affair," "A Childhood";

Kestrel: "Leaving Song," "The Singing";

Many Mountains Moving: "Good Girl," "Theodicy";

Northwest Review: "Last Call";

Ploughshares: "The Numbers";

Poetry International: "Fine," "Getting Older," "Ha";

The Prose Poem: "Last Gifts";

River City: "New Year's Day";

The Sun: "The Body In Extremis" (as "Metaphors for the Body In Extremis");

Tampa Review: "Blue Door," "Ranchos de Taos, August";

33 Review: "Nothing," "Spill";

Threepenny Review: "Glass," "Intimacy," "Quantum," "The Witness";

Willow Springs: "At Moss Beach," "Near Heron Lake."

The poems in the section "Blue Door" also previously appeared in a chapbook, *Dark Veil*, in *SEXTET ONE* from Pennywhistle Press. The following poems also appeared in anthologies and the editors are gratefully acknowledged: "Generations" in *American Diaspora: Poetry of Exile* (University of Iowa Press); "Like That" in *The Beacon Best of 1999: Creative Writing by Women and Men of All Colors* (Beacon Press); "Virgin Spring" in *The Best American Poetry 2000* (Scribner); "At Moss Beach" in *The Geography of Home: California's Poetry of Place* (Heyday Books); "Therapy" in *In the Palm of Your Hand: The Poet's Portable Workhop* (Tilbury House); "Intimacy" in *Night Out* (Milkweed Editions); "Theodicy" in *9mm: Poets Respond to Violence in America*; "Aliens" in *The Pushcart Prizes XXI*; "The Body In Extremis" (as "Metaphors for the Body In Extremis") in *Things Shaped In Passing: More "Poets for Life" Writing from the AIDS Pandemic* (Persea).

"Generations," "Night of the Living, Night of the Dead," "One-Night Stands," "Onset" (as "Likeness"), and "The Revered Poet Instructs Her Students on the Importance of Revision" were selected for the 1998 Chelsea Award for Poetry.

Thanks also to editors at the following Web sites for putting some of these poems on-line: *The Alsop Review*, *ForPoetry*, *In Sublette's Barn*, *PBS/Fooling With Words*, and *Poetry Daily*.

And especially: Dorianne Laux, Joe Millar, and Thom Ward for their critical attention; Robert Specter, Nancy Keane, and the regulars at the 3300 Club for helping me translate the photographs in my head; and Joey and Aya, whose love sustained me more than they knew.

ABOUT THE AUTHOR

Kim Addonizio is the author of two previous collections from BOA Editions, *The Philosopher's Club* and *Jimmy & Rita*. With Dorianne Laux, she co-authored *The Poet's Companion: A Guide to the Pleasures of Writing Poetry* (W.W. Norton). A book of stories, *In the Box Called Pleasure*, was published in 1999 by Fiction Collective 2. Her awards include two NEA Fellowships, a Commonwealth Club Poetry Medal, and a Pushcart Prize. She lives in San Francisco, where she freelances as a teacher of private workshops in the Bay Area. She recently joined the faculty of Goddard's low-residency MFA program. She can be found online at http: addonizio. home. mindspring. com.

BOA EDITIONS, LTD.

AMERICAN POETS CONTINUUM SERIES

Vol. 1 *The Fuhrer Bunker: A Cycle of Poems in Progress*
W. D. Snodgrass

Vol. 2 *She*
M. L. Rosenthal

Vol. 3 *Living With Distance*
Ralph J. Mills, Jr.

Vol. 4 *Not Just Any Death*
Michael Waters

Vol. 5 *That Was Then: New and Selected Poems*
Isabella Gardner

Vol. 6 *Things That Happen Where There Aren't Any People*
William Stafford

Vol. 7 *The Bridge of Change: Poems 1974–1980*
John Logan

Vol. 8 *Signatures*
Joseph Stroud

Vol. 9 *People Live Here: Selected Poems 1949–1983*
Louis Simpson

Vol. 10 *Yin*
Carolyn Kizer

Vol. 11 *Duhamel: Ideas of Order in Little Canada*
Bill Tremblay

Vol. 12 *Seeing It Was So*
Anthony Piccione

Vol. 13 *Hyam Plutzik: The Collected Poems*

Vol. 14 *Good Woman: Poems and a Memoir 1969–1980*
Lucille Clifton

Vol. 15 *Next: New Poems*
Lucille Clifton

Vol. 16 *Roxa: Voices of the Culver Family*
William B. Patrick

Vol. 17 *John Logan: The Collected Poems*

Vol. 18 *Isabella Gardner: The Collected Poems*

Vol. 19 *The Sunken Lightship*
Peter Makuck

Vol. 20 *The City in Which I Love You*
Li-Young Lee

Vol. 21 *Quilting: Poems 1987–1990*
Lucille Clifton

Vol. 22 *John Logan: The Collected Fiction*

Vol. 23 *Shenandoah and Other Verse Plays*
Delmore Schwartz

Vol. 24 *Nobody Lives on Arthur Godfrey Boulevard*
Gerald Costanzo

Vol. 25 *The Book of Names: New and Selected Poems*
Barton Sutter

Vol. 26 *Each in His Season*
W. D. Snodgrass

Vol. 27 *Wordworks: Poems Selected and New*
Richard Kostelanetz

Vol. 28 *What We Carry*
Dorianne Laux

Vol. 29 *Red Suitcase*
Naomi Shihab Nye

Vol. 30 *Song*
Brigit Pegeen Kelly

Vol. 31 *The Fuehrer Bunker: The Complete Cycle*
W. D. Snodgrass

Vol. 32 *For the Kingdom*
Anthony Piccione

Vol. 33 *The Quicken Tree*
Bill Knott

Vol. 34 *These Upraised Hands*
William B. Patrick

Vol. 35 *Crazy Horse in Stillness*
William Heyen

COLOPHON

Tell Me, poems by Kim Addonizio,
was set with Sabon and Hoefler Text Ornament fonts
by Richard Foerster, York Beach, Maine.
The jacket and covers were designed by
Lisa Mauro/Mauro Design, Rochester, New York.
Manufacturing was by McNaughton & Gunn,
Saline, Michigan.

Special support for this book came from the following
individuals and organizations:
Abraham Associates, Debra Audet, Susan DeWitt Davie,
Brad & Debra Dean, Richard Garth & Mimi Hwang,
Dane & Judy Gordon, Robert & Willy Hursh,
Archie & Pat Kutz, Deborah Ronnen,
Andrea & Paul Rubery, Pat & Michael Wilder,
Sabra Wood, Lorraine Vail.